5 KEYS TO LEADERSHIP
(Through the Eyes of Moses)

By
Chayla Cooper

For information address Sleeq Productions at:
SleeqProductions@Gmail.com

https://amzn.to/36On252

First Edition, First Print 2020
ISBNs:
-ebook: 978-0-9966605-7-0
-paperback: 978-0-9966605-8-7
-audiobook: 978-0-9966605-9-4

Summary:

From million dollar companies to local establishments, all successful businesses do one thing, serve. Whether that's a burger or a streaming service, service to the masses is what creates success. Even Jesus said, "whoever wants to become great among you must be your servant, and whoever wants to be first must be your slave just as the Son of Man did not come to be served, but to serve, and to give his life as a ransom for many." (Matthew 20:26-28)

In 5 Keys To Leadership (Through The Eyes Of Moses), you will discover:
- How to get buy-in from your team on any initiative
- How to supplement your weakness
- The best way to adapt to change
- The shocking action item that will improve your mental health

In a Barna Group survey of Christian adults, 64% stated that integrity as the most important trait for a leader to have. 5 Keys To Leadership (Through The Eyes Of Moses) will help you to dig deeper and become the leader that God has created you to be, even if you aren't religious as it covers concepts such as vision, delegation, communication, and more!

Ordering Information:

Quantity sales. Special discounts are available on quantity purchases by corporations, associations, and others. For details, contact publisher at the email above.

Dedicated to my Mother, Memo, and Papa
Thank you for nurturing and loving me into the woman I am today
I hope I make you proud

Table of Contents

CHAPTER 1
INTRODUCTION

L eadership has been a staple throughout the Bible. From God leading Adam on a walk through the garden of Eden, David leading men into victorious battle, Gideon leading his 300 against the Midianites, and of course the leader of Christianity itself, Jesus Christ showing us how to live according to the new covenant of God. Often referred to as sheep or a flock, it is evident that our Father in Heaven knows that we cannot be left alone to our own devices and places leaders in our lives to guide us along the way. The prophets of the old testament led the Hebrews in God's ways, King Solomon spoke wisdom to his people, and Jospeh exemplified forgiveness as second to pharaoh in Egypt. All leaders in their own right, but in the end, nothing without God's favor and guidance.

Leadership isn't just a box you check on your resume to show that you have supervisor experience, it's a calling for those who not only can step up to the plate, but who God uses to transform the lives of others. In 2018, INC. published an article showcasing that sixty percent of individuals who leave their jobs do so due to poor management. That's over half of the workforce leaving their job because of poor leadership. And the crazy thing about it is there is an entire industry built on how to become a better leader. Today's gurus like Tony Robins, Grant Cardone, and John Maxwell have made millions trying to help people become the best visions of themselves and lead others into success, and yet something is not clicking for there to be over 90,000 books on Amazon right now on the topic. So where is the disconnect? Why is turnover still so high? One word…God.

Deuteronomy 28:13 states, "The Lord will make you the head, not the tail. If you pay attention to the commands of the Lord your God that I give you this day and carefully follow them, you will always be at the top, never at the bottom." God created the heavens and the earth and the fullness thereof, if He created man, only He knows how to guide you to success. He wants us to be the head (a leader) and not the tail, He wants to give us the victory in every circumstance that we come across, He wants to unleash a fountain of blessings over your life so that you will not lack for anything, and through you, be a flowing river of light into the lives of others. It was in this revelation that I came across the story of Moses, someone who fought against their calling for so long to become one of the greatest leaders of the old testament.

We all know the Sunday school version of Moses' life; infant child placed on the Nile river to escape Pharaoh's grasp, lived in the palace as a prince of Egypt who eventually ran away, only to return and be used as God's vessel to lead the children of Israel to the promise land. But beyond the overview, Moses was human just like you and I. And as exciting as it must have been to lead a newly freed nation from over four hundred years of bondage, it came with its challenges. I can imagine his internal monologue, "How will they trust me? Am I doing this right? I have the vision but don't know where to go…what if they abandon the mission?" With all of the uncertainties that laid before him, one thing was constant, God's hand in his life.

5 Keys to Leadership Through the Eyes of Moses is a deep dive into the human and spiritual construct of leadership as it was designed. Showcasing practical tools and knowledge that God has for us, I hope this book opens your mind and heart to the various areas that you can improve

on as a leader. In order to succeed as a team, change always starts from the top down. Feel free to take notes, highlight, and doggy ear your way into becoming a better leader and take the steps to improve your team's culture. Now, let's lower that sixty percent together.

CHAPTER 2
PARTNERSHIP WITH GOD

Adam and Eve, David and Johnathan, and Elijah and Elisha are some of the partnerships that you'll find in the Bible. Community and companionship has always been God's plan for us. In Genesis 2:18 we find our Lord's thoughts regarding Adam being by himself, "It is not good for man to be alone. I will make a helper suitable for him." And to go even further back, during the creation we find God holding court with the divine trinity when He said, "let us make man in our image, in our likeness and let them rule over the fish of the sea and the birds of the air, over the livestock, over all the earth, and over all the creatures that move along the ground" (Genesis 1:26). If the Lord of Lords contains partnership, it is imperative that we understand that nothing can come to pass without the inclusion of others. So why not partner with the one who created the heavens and earth and has all authority in His hands? It is futile to try to succeed without God's grace over our plans, as it is through Him that abundance rains. 1 Corinthians 3:7 shares, "So neither the one who plants nor the one who waters is anything, but only God, who makes things grow." Though an old agricultural example, it still stands today. Laboring as hard as you can is great for your motivation, but motivation is only temporary, God's grace and supply is forever. And though you may feel like you don't need His help, God has been reaching out to partner with you from the very beginning of time and is speaking to you…if you would be still and listen.

Have you ever been in the market for a new car and did one search online, only to have ads pop up over and over again on Facebook and other social media platforms? Then on top of images bombarding you in your pocket, you're being stalked by your dream car in real life as well! No matter

4

where you go, how long your commute is, or where you park, you constantly see your dream car. Is there a computer chip implanted in your brain that knows when to show you certain products over and over to get you to buy? Maybe…but probably not. The manifestation in the physical world is due to your attention. Whether it be conscious or subconscious, your brain is paying attention to your surroundings and heightening your sense of awareness to show you what your heart desires. God is like this, He'll constantly show you something or put you in the same situations to teach you to hear His voice and rely on Him. It is imperative that you begin to learn how to discern your voice from that of the Lord's if you are going to be a leader.

Moses heard the voice of the Lord, just as the prophet Samuel did, and both times the men stated, "here I am", ready to do the will of the Lord. Are you ready and willing to do as the Lord commands whenever and however He presents himself? Nothing happens by chance, we're each a piece of thread that belongs in the grand tapestry that is God's great design.

Every time I received a promotion in my career or came into contact with someone new, I believed that I was placed there to serve a purpose and to learn something new myself. How to manage toxic relationships in a Christian manner, be still within myself, and speak faith into those that were discouraged around me were all lessons that I had to grasp within my adult career. Each morning that I stepped into my workplace I realized that despite my job title as a business analyst, consultant, or analyst, it all meant fell short to my main title as God's representative. Secured in that space and in that mindset, I knew that everywhere I stepped, I was a natural leader and no matter how tough it may get, I was never alone and could do more than I could imagine.

The beautiful thing about partnering with God is that God will do the heavy lifting in your life. The book of Exodus is a testament that God is capable of great wonders and will perform them on your behalf if you trust Him. Exodus 3:9 shares, "And now the cry of the Israelites has reached me, and I have seen the way the Egyptians are oppressing them. So now, go. I am sending you to Pharaoh to bring my people the Israelites out of Egypt." When the Israelites asked for freedom, God stepped out of time itself, stretched out His mighty hand and deliver ten plagues to convince Pharaoh to do so. After their release, the Hebrews wandered through the wilderness and complained about the lack of food in the desert. "The Lord said to Moses, 'I have heard the grumbling of the Israelites. Tell them, 'At twilight you will eat meat, and in the morning you will be filled with bread. Then you will know that I am the Lord your God.'" (Exodus 16:11-12). And of course being in a desert presents the challenge of where to find water, our God had that covered as well, "…Walk on ahead of the people. Take with you some of the elders of Israel and take in your hand the staff with which you struck the Nile, and go. I will stand there before you by the rock at Horeb. Strike the rock, and water will come out of it for the people to drink" (Exodus 17:5-6). Coinciding with the New Testament scripture, "Ask and it will be given to you; seek and you will find; knock and the door will be opened to you" (Matthew 7:7), our Lord is beyond gracious and will always provide for His children, so why not partner with him on your endeavors?

As a leader, you will face many obstacles within the workplace and though your title may allude that you know everything, as human beings, we don't. The constant pressure to perform at a high standard can lead many to feel stressed and overwhelmed. Seen as proud tattoos to show off as a sign of your leadership, many are left feeling as if they have to deal with these traits on their own…but you don't have to. Taking a moment to pray could not only give you the wisdom to lead those around you, but to provide you with a peace that you're not in this alone. God hears you and sees your work, and as you live your purpose with Him on your side, just as the Israelites, all you have to do is ask and seek God's face and He will handle your request in unbelievable ways.

There's a saying that, "success leaves clues". When referencing God, the children of Israel would often say that He was the God of Abraham, Issac, and Jacob (also known as Israel), indeed these were the nations forefathers, but most importantly, their stories were a testament to God's faithfulness to their lineage. God promised Abraham "I will make you into a great nation and I will bless you; I will make your name great, and you will be a blessing. I will bless those who bless you, and whoever curses you I will curse; and all peoples on earth will be blessed through you" (Genesis 12:2-3). Despite the moans and groans of the freed children of Israel in the wilderness, God was faithful to see them through because of the covenant He made with their ancestors. Things did not happen the way that they expected, on their timeline, or through the person they wanted, but God was faithful to them, despite their impatient actions. God is still shining His love and light on us through this covenant. Leaving us clues in His word that we will get through any trial that we may face, any mess that we may encounter, and any weapon that forms against us. You will succeed and through your partnership with God, blessings, abundance, and success have no choice but to flow to and from you.

CHAPTER 3

SUPPLEMENT YOUR WEAKNESSES

Craig Groeschel, founder of Life Church once said, "When you delegate tasks, you create followers. When you delegate authority, you create leaders." It is often a misconception that leaders should hold all authority and only relinquish tasks that they can't accomplish in their hectic day to their subordinates…but this does not build and empower those around you. A sign of a great leader is one who can leave the office for the day and know that it'll still be standing upon their return and running just as smooth, if not smoother than when they left it. Authority is the empowering factor that creates new ideas, challenges the status quo, and provides reassurance.

Upon receiving his assignment from the Lord, Moses was unsure if others would believe him and follow his direction. Instead of going to each and every Hebrew in Egypt and giving them a dream of Moses coming down a mountain to free them, God empowered Moses with wonders to show those who doubted who sent him.

"Then the Lord said to him, "What is that in your hand?"
"A staff," he replied.
The Lord said, "Throw it on the ground."
Moses threw it on the ground and it became a snake, and he ran from it.
Then the Lord said to him, "Reach out your hand and take it by the tail." So Moses reached out and took hold of the snake and it turned back into a staff in his hand. "This," said the Lord, "is so that they may believe that the Lord, the God of their fathers—the God of Abraham, the God of Isaac and the God of Jacob—has appeared to you."

Then the Lord said, "Put your hand inside your cloak." So Moses put his hand into his cloak, and when he took it out, the skin was leprous—it had become as white as snow.

"Now put it back into your cloak," he said. So Moses put his hand back into his cloak, and when he took it out, it was restored, like the rest of his flesh. Then the Lord said, "If they do not believe you or pay attention to the first sign, they may believe the second. But if they do not believe these two signs or listen to you, take some water from the Nile and pour it on the dry ground. The water you take from the river will become blood on the ground." (Exodus 4:2-9)

Leadership means providing the correct tools and structure for employees to ensure that they can succeed despite the obstacles they may face. By providing tools and showing your employees how to supplement their weaknesses in times of strife, you build their character and trust in you. As stated in the beginning of this book, well over sixty percent of the workforce leave positions due to management, but what if they were empowered, mentally fed, and poured into? What if they were nurtured and given room to grow in their field? As a leader, it is imperative that you sit down with your employees one by one and discuss their goals and ambitions in not only their career, but their personal life as well. As a supervisor, it is then your job to find ways to correlate those aspirations into tasks, lessons, and moments of authority that you can instill in them. That feeling of care and attentiveness will lead to doors not only opening for them, but for you as a leader. Imagine happy employees that commend you on your work, a work environment where ideas flow and everyone is striving for succession, a boss that looks to you in amazement as morale is evidently boosted, and even a promotion for yourself because others notice the peaceful and accomplished atmosphere that you bring to the table. Supplement your employee's weaknesses with the strength you have and let God do the rest.

After God provided Moses with authority to command the ears of his peers, He provided him with the tools he'll need to succeed. The first provision of wonders was meant to give Moses authority of his mind, equipping him with the leadership he'll need to convince the Hebrews to follow him. The second provision was given to assist with his physical limitation…his speech. Exodus 4:10-12 shares, "Moses said to the Lord, "Pardon your servant, Lord. I have never been eloquent, neither in the past nor since you have spoken to your servant. I am slow of speech and tongue." The Lord said to him, "Who gave human beings their mouths? Who makes them deaf or mute? Who gives them sight or makes them blind? Is it not I, the Lord? Now go; I will help you speak and will teach you what to say." The Lord is sovereign. Our Father knows what tools we need to accomplish our purpose, and as we lack for nothing in Him, God already made a way for Moses to fulfill all that he was commanded. Despite the fear, God pushed Moses to believe in himself and the Lord's ability to see him through. Does your team know that they can count on you in times of uncertainty? Do they know that despite all that may arise in their day, you have provided them with the resources they'll need to succeed?

Though we may appear impeccable in our own eyes, we are not perfect beings and reflection is always great for our growth. We are called to be the church in the world and to light up the darkness with God's love everywhere we go. As leaders we should be able to empower those around us and ensure that they have no fear, doubt, or insecurity about their abilities. Remember, God didn't give us these traits, only power, love, and a strong mind. Guide your team to the best of your ability, and where you feel that you fall short, know that it is in God's design that our weakness is tied to His strength.

You can always find God's reassurance to rest and rely on Him whenever you hit a stumbling block. Jeremiah 1:5 and 8, " 'Before I formed you in the womb I knew you, before you were born I set you apart…Do not be afraid of them, for I am with you and will rescue you,' declares the Lord." Judges 6:14 states, "The Lord turned to him and said, "Go in the strength you have and save Israel out of Midian's hand. Am I not sending you?" And Proverbs 3:5-6 tells us to, "Trust in the Lord with all your heart; and lean not unto your own understanding. In all your ways acknowledge Him, and He will direct your paths." God knows who you are, where you are, what you need, and when you need it. It is in Him that we truly have supply for our weaknesses. And no, He may not turn the office coffee into wine or make the conference table rise from the floor unexpectedly, but our Father uses situations, circumstances, and individuals around you to provide you with a physical representation of His helping hand.

Moses, concerned with his slow speech, feared that not only would he not be able to convey the Lord's message clearly for those to hear, but I assume he worried about his reputation as well. The thought of standing before his peers, stammering over his words, and being ridiculed probably stopped Moses in his tracks, but as always, God provided an aid to him. "But Moses said, "Pardon your servant, Lord. Please send someone else." Then the Lord's anger burned against Moses and he said, "What about your brother, Aaron the Levite? I know he can speak well. He is already on his way to meet you, and he will be glad to see you. You shall speak to him and put words in his mouth; I will help both of you speak and will teach you what to do. He will speak to the people for you, and it will be as if he were your mouth and as if you were God to him" (Exodus 4:13-16). Delegating

11

authority may create leaders, but just as Mr. Groeschel stated, delegating task creates followers, and this is exactly what Moses needed to rally the nation to depart from Egypt. With Moses delegating oration to Aaron, he could focus on gaining the right insight and direction from the Lord. Are you utilizing your strongest employees to gain allies and followers for your mission?

Often when there's a change in policy, procedure, and leadership within a unit or company there are three classes of people that can either make or break the transition; the champions, the fence-sitters, and the cynics. The champions are the ones who are excited for the change to happen, they can't wait to see how things will turn out, and they're the company's cheerleaders. The fence-sitters or acceptors are just…here. They don't particularly care which way the wind blows as long as they still have a job at the end of the day. And then there are your cynics, also known as your critics. These individuals are extremely resistant to change, have something negative to say about any and everything, and will do their best to drag others down with them. This group of people can't wait to say, "I told you so". I'm sure you've dealt with these three groups of people when you conveyed new changes and challenges coming down the pipeline. As a leader, it is imperative that when you are asking people to adjust to change, that you lean on the champions on your team. Change is scary, but these champions will encourage others to power through to the goal line, assist others where they may need help, and increase the team's morale when the tough times arise. These people are the life blood of any team and can "rally the troops" for you when it's time to fulfill the mission.

All in all, delegation is the key to not only your success as a leader, but as a team. I know this can be hard trait to grasp for people, trust me. I would rather do so many things on my own to ensure that they are completed correctly, than to delegate and have to do double work and retrace another person's errors, but in doing so, how will I gain the time to do the important things in my day? How can I nurture the leaders within my team? How can I supplement my weakness so as to ensure that we succeed as a group? And above all, how can I hear God's voice and comprehend my next steps if I am tied down by things that don't need my immediate attention? God has provided us with the tools and personnel to accomplish not only our earthly goals, but heavenly assignment as well. If we don't utilize all that He has given us, how do we plan on succeeding? We can't. Trust your team.

CHAPTER 4
ADAPT TO CHANGE

Leadership is futile without change. Imagine this, you don't supervise children as they watch a movie, you may watch it with them, but you're not there as an authoritarian in that moment. But when they go into the front yard to play you make sure that you're watching them, ensuring their safety, and guiding them. The change in environment, threats, and outside influences distract your children and it is your job to keep them focused enough to have fun within the parameters of your property. Change is a badge on the uniform of every leader. How you guide your team during this period, how you grow from the experience, and what lessons you learn from it are pivotal to your success.

Moses experienced so many changes in his life that it ultimately brought out the strength and perseverance he needed to shape his leadership style and guide the children of Israel. From prince of Egypt, to murderer, to a man on the run, to shepherd, to his organizing of the Hebrews as God punished Egypt, leading them through the Red Sea, to guiding Israel through the wilderness, to seeing the next generation walk into the promise land, each transition in his life required a new level of trust within the Lord and a look within himself. But the first thing that Moses had to do before he could become one of the greatest leaders to echo through the pages of history was to forgive himself.

Conflict arises in the fact that we have competing ideals that we struggle with. Should I write this employee up, or should I coach them and train them up to their potential? Can I finish this project on time with the constant pull from urgent concerns that need my attention? Do I let the

14

negative individual of my team remain here due to their tenure, or do I let them go because they're holding the team back? These are all hard questions that you have to internalize and decipher and sometimes the aftermath will result in you feeling uncomfortable, uncertain, and even receiving backlash from your employees...but are you willing to trust the process? Are you willing to trust God?

Moses balanced on the razors edge of am I a prince of Egypt bound by traditions and expectations or am I a child of the Hebrew people who I watch get beaten everyday with no consequence to myself? This uncertainty of identity led him to murdering one of the guards in defense of his people. Exodus 2:11-15 shares, "One day, after Moses had grown up, he went out to where his own people were and watched them at their hard labor. He saw an Egyptian beating a Hebrew, one of his own people. Looking this way and that and seeing no one, he killed the Egyptian and hid him in the sand. The next day he went out and saw two Hebrews fighting. He asked the one in the wrong, 'Why are you hitting your fellow Hebrew?' The man said, 'Who made you ruler and judge over us? Are you thinking of killing me as you killed the Egyptian?' Then Moses was afraid and thought, 'What I did must have become known.' When Pharaoh heard of this, he tried to kill Moses, but Moses fled from Pharaoh and went to live in Midian..."

Moses' complexity of identity within himself forced him to act out, though with good intentions, in a bad manor. The abrupt change in circumstances not only exiled him from his own people, but from the only home he knew. It is this same pain, confusion, and uncertainty within himself that leads Moses to discount the fact that God wants to use him to free his people. Questions like "What if they don't believe me?", "Can you send another?", and "What will I say?" are all seeds of inner doubt that

15

lingered from the pain of his past that he refused to let go. Pain so deep that when the Lord of Lord's asks him to move on His behalf, Moses diminishes his abilities.

You must forgive yourself for your past actions in order to give God the ability to use you how He chooses. Isaiah 43:19 tells us that God is doing a new thing. Psalm 55:22 shares that we should cast our burdens on the Lord and He will sustain us. 1 Peter 5:7 reads for us to cast all of our anxiety on him because he cares. The bible gives us reassurance after reassurance that our God is for us and not against us. He is the author of change and forgiveness and in the end, his purpose will always prevail (Proverbs 19:21). It's not a question of are you good enough for God to use, but rather, do you forgive yourself for how you handled past situations and can you trust in the Lord to guide you as He fulfills His purpose and plan? Let it go. You are stopping the flow of miracles that God wants to get to you and through you.

Moses' story is also a great reminder that where you start is not where you will end up and with each change of season, a different style of leadership will be required. Have you ever taken a leadership style quiz or a career strength assessment? It seems that these are all the rage now, answering questions to dissect how you navigate through the business world. But my problem with these quizzes is once they're taken, the results tend to be thrown to the wind. There's the initial excitement of sharing your results with your colleagues of where you fall on the spectrum, but no one utilizes the data to actually ensure that their team is functioning based on the strengths that were discovered. This leads to miscommunication, misinterpretation, and ultimately low morale because employees feel as if they aren't understood and functioning at their highest capacity. I can honestly tell you that in my well over ten years of professional service that

16

I was asked one time what leadership style do I prefer? My jaw physically dropped in awe. I literally stopped the interview to tell my potential supervisor thank you for asking me that question. I explained that I prefer a more hands off approach (laissez-faire) as we're all adults and when hired to do a job, I trust that the supervisor believes that I'm capable of fulfilling my duties to the team. Though I can adequately pull my weight to support the team, that doesn't negate the fact that I also have supervisor and leadership experience myself, and can lead a group of people to ensure tasks are completed correctly and on time. This pendulum swing of experiences proves that I have gone through phases in my life where I was a cog in the machine that helped the business run smoothly to leading the charge of innovation. My ability to shift and change not only helped me climb the ranks quickly, but has led me to this one moment in time where I was seeking more responsibility, more experiences, and dare I say it…more change. It is that willingness to accept the uncertain and adapt to circumstances that reassures me that I am being molded for my destiny.

God has a funny way of taking our pain and past experiences and using them in latter seasons as weapons for His kingdom. So many verses come to mind in regards to this notion; Romans 8:28, "And we know that in all things God works for the good of those who love him, who have been called according to his purpose." Philippians 1:6, "being confident of this, that he who began a good work in you will will carry it on to completion until the day of Christ Jesus." Psalm 138:8, "The Lord will work out his plans for my life— for your faithful love, O Lord, endures forever…" These reassurances of God's love and purpose for us as we navigate this winding road called life lets us know that everything will be alright. As He continues to instill peace of mind through His word, place all of your fears in His hands because He is faithful to complete all that He has started.

With tears flowing from her eyes, Moses' mother, Jochebed, placed her son in a basket on the Nile River, uncertain of his final destination. When she relinquished control of her infant son, she trusted the Father to place him somewhere safe from the persecution surrounding her. That seed of faith led to her being summoned to work in Pharaoh's palace to care for the very child she released to back to God (Exodus 2:3-9). As Moses fled from Pharaoh's grasp into the wilderness, God not only showed him mercy to make it through the desert, but allowed him the gift of time to heal from his pain and to find a sense of family among the Midianites (Exodus 2: 21-22). While standing in defiance of his past, Moses finished what he started years ago and fought for the Hebrew people and their deliverance from bondage. God took every piece of pain, confusion, and exile and redeemed it for His good and the good of His children. What looked like dead ends and failure, turned into roses on the grave of disappointment. Unexpected changes in circumstances aren't necessarily the end of your world, but the seeds of destiny that God will revisit when it best serves you.

I recall the time I was an assistant manager and I felt that the work I was doing was mundane and for someone less qualified than my talents and education. I felt superior in my mindset, yet I also felt stuck in my circumstance. One particular instance, my supervisor told me that she wanted to know the root cause of why so many individuals were missing their appointments with the office; was there a particular person not calling their clients, were we not vetting the applications correctly, or was our system in need of an overhaul? I pulled from our system's database how many missed appointments we had for that previous month and there was over seven hundred! I was expected to dig into each case and find the common denominator, along with my normal duties, and whatever popped up throughout the day. As you can guess, I was not pleased. This task, coupled with running down other supervisors for reports and handling conflict in and outside of the office, had me at my wit's end and ready to quit. It wasn't until I got the unexpected call to interview for a manager position that I realized that everything I was doing was just preparation for my future. My "senseless" navigating of reports was actually God honing my data analytics skills. My headaches of dealing with irate customers was God teaching me patience and problem solving. My chasing down of superiors was God's way of teaching me to plan ahead and improve my time management skills. Everything I was enduring and complaining about was God's way of fortifying me in the wilderness for the journey He was taking me on. Zechariah 4:10 states, "Do not despise these small beginnings, for the Lord rejoices to see the work begin…" This passage has helped me manage many days where I felt that I was above the task I was completing and humbled me to the notion that God isn't always the bombastic thunderous voice from the heavens when He asks you to do something. Sometimes, it's the small whisper to buy your coworker's lunch, the extra grace you give your employee for being late when you know they just had a new baby and sleep has escaped from them, or the mundane report that you have to turn in weekly to track the progress of the unit. Every step you take is a part of your destiny. No matter how small it may be, always remember that forward…is still forward.

That's not to say that change won't hurt, it definitely will. Just as lifting weights tears down your muscles to gain strength, God will stretch you pass your comfort zone to push you into the next level. It will hurt your pride, your ego, your head, and even your heart…but who you will become when you look back over His work in your life will be far worth it. Moses' pain of mis-identity led to his exile and being a foreigner in a strange land. From prince to pauper, he lived a life of uncertainty while on the run. Is my family still alive? Am I still being hunted for my crimes? How can I really enjoy this new life when I know my community is suffering? The mental anguish he experienced surely kept him up many nights. And then to be called by the Lord of Lords to go back to Egypt to defy a man who he once called brother…the anxiety that ran through his body caused him to come up with every excuse as to why he wasn't fit to fulfill his mission. But with each disappointment he felt in his physical world, he experienced favor, grace, and a deeper connection with his heavenly Father.

But if you truly want to see the shift of God in your everyday actions, you must master this one feat…control your anger. Controlling your anger increases your spiritual stamina and enables you to think through any situation clearly, removing emotions and allowing logic to reign. That's not to say that anger isn't a human emotion that won't come and go, but it's a response triggered by fear, the unknown, and abrupt change in the status quo. 2 Timothy 1:7 reminds us that God has not given us a spirit of fear, but of power, love, and a sound mind (self-discipline and self-control in some translations). Fear, as with change, is inevitable and something that can't be escaped, but your reaction to it is always within your control.

The book of Numbers continues the story of the nation of Israel after their release from Egypt as they wander through the wilderness. Without water to sustain them, the congregation complains to Moses and Aaron as to why they are being subjected to such pain, when they had such abundance in Egypt along the Nile. The two brothers take the nation's petition to the Lord and Moses is told, "'Take the staff, and you and your brother Aaron gather the assembly together. Speak to that rock before their eyes and it will pour out its water. You will bring water out of the rock for the community so they and their livestock can drink.' So Moses took the staff from the

20

Lord's presence, just as he commanded him." (Numbers 20:8-9). It's what happened next that cancelled the promise over their lives. "He and Aaron gathered the assembly together in front of the rock, and Moses said to them, 'Listen, you rebels, must we bring you water out of this rock?' Then Moses raised his arm and struck the rock twice with his staff. Water gushed out, and the community and their livestock drank. But the Lord said to Moses and Aaron, "Because you did not trust in me enough to honor me as holy in the sight of the Israelites, you will not bring this community into the land I give them.""

It's easy to read these passages and skip over the true reason Moses and his brother were denied entrance into the promise land. When hearing the nation's petition for water, God told Moses to "tell" the rock to bring forth water, but in front of the people, Moses "struck" the rock with his staff twice out of frustration. One act of anger caused a dream to perish, forfeiting the promise of the Lord. This same notion can be translated into the business world. As a leader, it is your job to navigate the choppy waters with strength and resilience as the team looks to you for peace in the storm. An outburst of anger may get you the result that you asked for, as it got Moses the water from the rock, but it will leave a damaging effect on you and your team. The main consequence being that they'll always remember how you made them feel in a time of pressure. This new found level of distrust can lead to a lack of communication, lower morale, or an exodus outside of your unit or company.

Remember God has a funny way of taking our pain and past experiences and using them in latter seasons as weapons for His kingdom. If you fast forward to the new testament, you'll find that God replays the scene of his terrified children in the wilderness and provides a better

21

response from Jesus. This juxtaposition shows us the correct manner to act under pressure. Mark 4:35-41 is where we find Jesus and the disciples on a boat when a furious storm arises. As the boat sways back and forth, sizable waves crashed down on the disciples causing them to believe that they surely were going to die. All this panic and chaos occurred while Jesus slept peacefully in the stern. Terrified for their lives, they finally woke him up, but in such a tone that proved their distrust and anger in the moment, "Teacher, don't you care if we drown?" Instead of retorting in anger, throwing a rock at the sea, or telling them to leave him alone, Jesus got up and said to the wind and the waves, "Quiet! Be Still!" And all became silent and calm. He then turned to his disciples and asked them a question so close to what the father asked Moses, "Do you still have no faith?" After all the trials they overcame and miracles he performed, they still lacked faith, just as the Hebrews lacked faith in the God that delivered them from the hands of Pharaoh. Shouts of anger only show that you are not in control and you don't have faith in the orchestrator of your destiny or the outcome of the situation. Control your anger in all situations and leave such a reputation that your employees can believe that in the midst of fear, change, and uncertainty you have guided them before, and you'll guide them again.

CHAPTER 5

BELIEVE IN YOUR MISSION

When you get in your car you don't sit there and say, "wherever you decide to take me is where I'll go." Before you reach the car, you've already decided where you wanted to go, dressed for the occasion, and maybe even utilized a navigation app to determine the fastest route to reach your destination. Just as you took the time to plan out your day, this should be the case for your personal goals, as well as the goals for your team. Proverbs 29:18 tells us that "where there is no vision, the people perish...", when was the last time you wrote down where you wanted to go career wise, as a leader, or as a team? A vision written down becomes a plan and a plan initiates action, but you must first decide where you want to take your talents before you can see it in your sight. This simple step, along with your faith in the Father, will be your anchor to sustain you when things get tough.

Picture this, Moses awakes to a new day, basking in the peace of the palace walls among his belongings as fresh food is brought to him. This bliss quickly becomes distorted by the sound of wailing and lashings outside as slaves are being beaten while they labor in the sweltering Egyptian heat. A slap back to reality, Moses internally grapples with the notion that he is an orphan; a child not of royal blood and not fully welcomed into the nation of his forefathers. Eating away at him day in and day out, Moses finally picks a side in a moment of passion. Killing an Egyptian guard for striking a Hebrew, he buries the body in the sand to avoid his shame and punishment, and to show his solidarity with the Israelites...only to be mocked by these very people in the end. An act of impulse led Moses down a path that he did not plan for nor was he ready for all that was in store for him.

Our God is sovereign and has accounted for our mistakes within His holy plan. Moses didn't plan to kill a guard and run for his life when he woke up that morning. He didn't plan on meeting a tribe in the desert, marrying, and having children while in exile. He surely didn't plan on leaving his pampered palace life to become accustomed to a humbled reality, but God used it all to prepare him for the purpose He had for his life...the same is done for you.

Have you ever did something for the right reason, but when you looked back on the situation, you regretted the way you handled things? This could be gossiping about a lazy employee prior to you terminating them. It may seem like no harm-no foul now that their gone, but the words from your mouth have now illicit an atmosphere of distrust and poor communication within your team. What about a personal relationship where instead of simply talking about your differences with your significant other and finding a solution, you decided to shut down and ignore their feelings for the temporary satisfaction of being right? Without a clear vision, you'll be wandering around in the dark and seeking immediate gratification from anything that imitates light. But if your course is charted out, you can return to it, read it, and imprint it on your heart to know that your work is not in vain and that you have an ultimate purpose to fulfill and each step that you take towards it is an accomplishment.

Just like Joseph with his dreams, David against Goliath, Gideon and his army, and Moses with his assignment, your mission is your own and you have to be prepared for others to fight you along the way because they weren't given the same assignment as you. Are you strong enough to withstand opposition, even though you know it's for the betterment of those around you? Leaders are individuals that are set apart and given the most daunting tasks not because they are the strongest warriors in God's kingdom and can bury their emotions deep to get the job done, but because of their ability to allow God to utilize them and acknowledge that when they are weak, God has the opportunity to show up and show out. Each of these men have faults that others would use to discount them as leaders; Joseph was the youngest of his family, a slave, and jailed as a rapist. David also was the youngest of his brothers, had no military background, and was discounted by his own father when the prophet Samuel was sent to anoint the next king from his household. Gideon had low self esteem, was the youngest in his family, and was constantly ridiculed by those around him. And of course Moses was the youngest of his siblings (Hebrew and within the palace), a murderer, and was slow of speech (believed to have a stutter). As you see, our God likes to take the least among us, the counted out, and social outcast to catapult His people to the next level of victory. You don't have to be the youngest in your family to be used, but if you're able to hear the whisper of the Lord and hold onto the mission He gave you despite everything you see, then God can use that faith and trust to bring miracles to pass.

Moses knew that he would be met with opposition from the Israel nation when he received his mission from the Lord and asked "What if they do not believe me or listen to me…" (Exodus 4:1). Despite the wonders that God provided him with and those seen before their eyes, each step into their promise was competing with the two steps they would take backwards at every turn.

After being led through the Red Sea, provided fresh manna every morning, on their way to the promise land and witnessing the presence of the Lord come down and shake mountains to be among His people, Moses went up to Mount Sinai to receive the ten commandments where the first two laws given were, "I am the Lord your God, who brought you out of Egypt, out of the land of slavery. You shall have no other gods before me. You shall not make yourself an image in the form of anything in heaven above or on the earth beneath or in the waters below. You shall not bow down to them or worship them; for I, the Lord your God, am a jealous God, punishing the children for the sin of the parents to the third and fourth generation of those who hate me, but showing love to a thousand generation of those who love me and keep my commandments" (Exodus 20:2-6). But upon his descent from the mountain, the first thing that Moses encounters is that his brother, Aaron, has led the nation of Israel in creating a golden calf to idolize and claim that it was this man made god that rescued them from the hands of Egypt. Disheartened, Moses had to beg God not to destroy them in the wilderness so as to not be a mockery to the other nations, "the Egyptians [would] say, 'It was with evil intent that he (God) brought them out, to kill them in the mountains and to wipe them off the face of the earth'..."(Exodus 32:12).

And even though they were spared from the hands of Pharaoh, shown wonders and saved from God's wrath at the mountain, the nation of Israel still had little faith when brought to the land that God had promised them. Upon sending 12 scouts to navigate the land, they returned with glorious fruit so large that two men had to carry a single vine of grapes. Reporting that the land was "indeed a bountiful country —a land flowing with milk and honey" (Numbers 13:27), they retracted into their timid shells when they referenced the people inhabiting the land as powerful and strong giants who would devour them. "Why is the Lord taking us to this country only to have us die in battle? Our wives and our little ones will be carried off as plunder! Wouldn't it be better for us to return to Egypt?" Then they plotted among themselves, "Let's choose a new leader and go back to

Egypt!" (Numbers 14:3-4). Despite the camps cries of distrust echoing throughout the camp, two of the scouts, Caleb and Joshua, stood with Moses and rebuked the notion that God has brought them this far to lead them into a path of destruction. "Do not rebel against the Lord, and don't be afraid of the people of the land. They are only helpless prey to us! They have no protection, but the Lord is with us! Don't be afraid of them!"(Numbers 14:9).

As a leader you will encounter opposition from every side; outside of your team, within your team, and within yourself. You must continue to press forward with the vision despite the opposition that you'll face on a daily basis from your fear, colleagues, and environment. Remember that faith is the evidence of things hoped for but not yet seen. You must take the vision that God has given you and before you take action, I want you to take inventory of how far He has brought you through your career and even your life. You are not where you were a decade ago, and you're truly not who you were even a year ago. He has been faithful to allow you to have some wins, but even more so to let His vision come to pass. Take action with the grounding that if God has brought you this far, then there is no telling what great joys await you on the other side of your trials.

And yes, carrying the burden of guiding others with their own ideals of what success may look like will be hard, but just as the scouts had to use two men to carry a vine of grapes from enemy territory, you will need a few people on your team to help carry the load of your vision as well. Have a mentor to guide you through uncharted waters, someone who has been where you are and is where you are striving to be in your career. God knew where the Hebrews were and the exact route needed to get them to the promise land. He saw the victory ahead of them, but it was their own shortsightedness that took what would have been an eleven day journey in the wilderness and turned it into a forty year pile of chaos and confusion. A mentor will help you avoid unnecessary pitfalls and distractions on your way to your promise because they've experienced the challenges and know how to navigate around them. Just as we deploy GPS on our journey through the streets, utilize the tutelage of a wiser colleague to take you to your calling.

Have a team ally that will speak to your employees on your behalf when you're not in the room. Aaron was this person for Moses throughout their guiding the nation out of Egypt, but soon succumbed to the pressure when Moses was away for too long. Have someone strong in conviction that knows how far your company and team has come and that nothing in front of them will stand in the way of the teams success. Aaron could not be trusted after he led the efforts in building an alter to a false god. It wasn't until years later that Caleb and Joshua became the face of the mission as they rebuked those that came against the Lord's promise to them. You will need this extra boost of morale, faith, and tenacity when times get hard. Even on the days that you find it difficult to get out of bed and keep pushing forward, have this backup system of encouragement waiting for you when enter the office. The infamous saying, "sometimes you have to encourage yourself" is very true as self motivation is a key to seeing the vision come to pass, but it is also true that we weren't meant to do life alone and having an ally, a friend in the trenches, will always push you to the excellence you may not see in yourself. Believe in your mission, believe in your team, believe in yourself, and above all…believe if God has given you a vision, He'll see you through its completion.

CHAPTER 6

PREPARE TO SACRIFICE

There's a social media challenge online where children have their favorite snack placed in front of them and then told by their parents that they can't touch it until they get back. The parent will go off screen for about two to three minutes with the child sitting there anticipating their return, sometimes patiently... sometimes with anxiousness. When the parent returns, the child is met with praise for showing restraint and given their snack as a reward. As adorable and funny as it may seem to watch, it amuses me that adults fail this same experiment when God asks us to wait on Him.

Children have the innate understanding that their parents won't leave them, will give them what they promise, and know that they'll be rewarded for their obedience. The small sacrifice in time doesn't compare to the pleasure of getting what they truly crave. Somewhere along our journey into adulthood, the concepts of sacrifice and patience has left our hearts. Consumed by the technology that lingers at our fingertips, we have grown accustomed to instant satisfaction in all areas of our life. We walk into restaurants with our orders waiting for us on a shelf, we send money effortlessly on our couch to one another, and God forbid a movie takes 2.5 seconds to buffer on our phones! We'll huff and puff and maybe even throw in a slight tantrum about how slow the wi-fi is. We weren't designed to have everything we wanted right away because it teaches us not to have patience, not to rely on the Father, and to short change ourselves from the mighty blessings we could get if we would wait on the Lord. Exodus 7:5 shows this beautifully when God tells Moses to go speak to Pharaoh a second time, "You are to say everything I command you, and your brother Aaron is to tell Pharaoh to let the Israelites go out of his country. But I will harden Pharaoh's heart, and though I multiply my signs and wonders in Egypt, he will not listen to you. Then I will lay my hand on Egypt and with mighty acts of judgment I will bring out my divisions, my people the Israelites. And the Egyptians will know that I am the Lord when I stretch out my hand against Egypt and bring the Israelites out of it." The Lord could have easily struck down Pharaoh in his sleep and the Israelites could have been released that very night, but God wanted a message to be embedded not only in their hearts, but their captors as well for generations to come. By patiently making them wait to see the wonders He would perform, the Hebrews would know that they were delivered by a mighty God who cared for them and not by their own works. This sacrifice of time and restraint led to the greatest deliverance that man still celebrates to this day; passover.

As a leader, the term sacrifice is commonly associated with pain, time, and money. If someone calls in for the day, you'll have to adjust your schedule to handle the extra workload that you weren't anticipating. When a worldwide pandemic appears out of nowhere and business decreases significantly, the tumultuous feeling of letting employees go to stay afloat can weigh heavy on your mind. Even making that dreaded phone call to your child to let them know you won't be at their game can be seen as a sacrifice for the success of the team. Though these are common depictions in the workplace, seldom does the term relationship come to mind.

Each individual that you employ, mentor, or work with not only bring their talents to the team, but they are a part of the overall culture. There is an unspoken trust that everyone shares, that despite any personal issues that may arise, the job will get done and it'll be done to the best of their ability. Every person is a cog in the wheel of the team. Remove one piece and you may not see the immediate effects, but you'll definitely feel the presence of it's absence. You may see a frequently late employee, but your employees may see a mentor and emotional coach. You may see a poor statistical performer, but you could be losing the best presenter and project manager on your team. This all ties into my earlier statement of evaluating the strengths of your team and seeing how they fit in the overall grand design of the company. You have to dig deeper than what your vision sees to ensure that you aren't throwing away what your team needs. Remember that Moses may have received the mission from God, but it was Aaron who supplemented his weakness of stuttering and spoke to Pharaoh and the Hebrews on his behalf. Don't sacrifice your culture for your temporary emotions, it could result in distrust and strife within your team and then no one would be productive and move the company forward.

Now that's not to say that there won't be legitimate reasons to replace a team member for the betterment of the company, but again that's why you as a leader must lead with spiritual wisdom and set your earthly emotions aside to accomplish the greater good. As Moses came down from Mount Sinai and meeting with the Lord, he discovered that his brother led the anticipating nation into building a false idol to worship due to Moses taking longer than they expected on the mountainside. "Aaron answered: Don't be angry with me. You know as well as I do that they are determined to do evil. They even told me, 'That man Moses led us out of Egypt, but now we don't know what has happened to him. Make us a god to lead us.' Then I asked them to bring me their gold earrings. They took them off and gave them to me. I threw the gold into a fire, and out came this bull. Moses knew that the people were out of control and that it was Aaron's fault. And now they had made fools of themselves in front of their enemies." (Exodus 32:22-25)

31

Not only was Aaron Moses' second in command, his voice to the masses, and confidant, he was his brother. The familial bond that tied him to his roots and and who God also chose to assist in delivering their people from bondage. This betrayal must have stung deeper than anything after all they had been through, but Moses, as humble as he was notated to be (Numbers 12:3), not only sacrificed a part of his emotional relationship with his brother, but that day over three thousand people were killed as atonement for their sin against the Lord. Though Aaron continued to assist Moses, imagine the sacrifice of lives and pain that was left on the rest of the camp because Aaron couldn't stand strong in the face of mounting pressure when placed in charge?

Sacrifices are bound to come in the form of relationships, time, and resources, but the ultimate stamp of a leader is that you'll be ok being left behind for the mission to succeed. As a supervisor your duty is to the company and the bottom line, but it is also to nurture your employees and build them up so much that they will either gain a higher position within the company or grow into their own fulfillment outside of the agency. If you have the same employees you started with twenty years ago, your team, along with yourself, is stagnant and won't reach their true potential personally or professionally.

In my career in the public sector, I promoted six times within ten years, always striving to gain the most knowledge I could from my current position. When given the chance to supervise my own team, I trained my employees on how I processed cases, handled complaints, and the clever ways I would remember policy…after all, I was one of the most decorated employee of the region for several years. My ultimate goal, for those that wanted it, was for them to not feel stagnant, but gain the tools they would need to step into the purpose God had for them. Whether that meant climbing the ranks of the agency and becoming an official at the State Office level or gaining methodologies for outside employment, I wanted to give them the best or nothing at all. I sacrificed my time, my secrets, my emotions to ensure that not only the mission of the agency was being upheld, but the mission that God placed on my heart to lead them to the best of my ability. Whether they elevated within the company or gained the courage to step out in faith, I was proud that their mission was being pushed forward. Though they were leaving me physically, they remained in my heart and mind and I knew that wherever they were, they were successful.

After killing a man, running from Pharaoh, witnessing God's wonders, walking his people through the red sea and wilderness, seeing God face to face, teaching the Hebrews the laws for which God wished for them to live by and constantly trying to keep the nation from rebelling, Moses did not get to walk into the promise land. I know, the most anticlimactic thing to say after his entire journey, but as I stated, we each play a part in the grand design of the Lord's story and you have to be ok knowing that you may have to pass the baton to someone else to finish the race.

Of course this book isn't that long and I implore you to take the time to read the entire story of the Israelite's deliverance from Egypt to the promise land on your own, but a constant theme you will see is that the nation constantly doubted God no matter how many miracles He performed. And as humble as Moses was and how hard he tried to lead the people to their birthright, his anger got the best of him. Remember in Numbers 20:10-13 Moses struck the rock out of anger of the Hebrews constantly complaining to him. The Lord said to both Aaron and Moses, "Because you did not believe in me, to uphold me as holy in the eyes of the people of

Israel, therefore you shall not bring this assembly into the land that I have given them." And just like a child chastised by their parent, Moses continued to serve and do as he was told, occasionally asking God to change His mind on the matter. It wasn't until the next book, Deuteronomy, that God gives Moses his final answer, "That is enough," the Lord said. "Do not speak to me anymore about this matter. Go up to the top of Pisgah and look west and north and south and east. Look at the land with your own eyes, since you are not going to cross this Jordan. But commission Joshua, and encourage and strengthen him, for he will lead this people across and will cause them to inherit the land that you will see." (Deuteronomy 3:26)

Are you willing to sacrifice your personal happiness to ensure that your team makes it into the promise land? Are you prepared to look at the big picture and remove your emotions from the equation to ensure that you are feeding those around you? Being a leader will have it's ups and downs but through it all you must stay vigilant to your purpose, watch your anger, build your culture, and train others for the mission that God has for them. Do this…and watch how prepared and blessed your life will become.

CHAPTER 7

ACTION ITEMS

There you have it, the five keys you must have to be an effective leader as illustrated through the old testament character Moses. To recap, you must first partner with God in all that you do. Though success leaves clues, God speaks to us and guides us on the path we should follow and more often than not, He does the heavy lifting to get the job done. Supplement your weaknesses by surrendering your problems to the one who is always your strength when you need it. Be able to adapt to change, for as Isaiah 43:19 states, "Behold, I am doing a new thing!" Our Father is a God of change and advancement, and does not like us to get used to complacency. Believe in your mission even when it goes against everything that you see and are used to. And of course, the ultimate test of a leader is that they are prepared to sacrifice. Each key dives into the fundamental business principles of communication, delegation, courage, vision, and sacrifice. To become the leader that you are called to be, you must master and balance all of these concepts.

Action items for improved communication:

1. Seek God every morning as you wake. Being in His presence acknowledges that you know He is the beginning of all things, the orchestrator of all things, and the peace before a chaotic day. Still your heart and mind each morning with prayer, worship, mediation, and maybe even the reading or hearing of His word. It is said that the cross has two beams, one going vertical and one going horizontal. The vertical one is the longest and represents our connection to the Father, while the horizontal one represents our connection to those around us. Getting into God's presence

before connecting with others will give you the peace to deal with the unexpected, speak to others in a more empathetic fashion, and hear the guidance needed to push onward when it seems tough.

2. Now that we're partnered with our heavenly Father, reach out to your team and actively listen to them on the issues that not only plague them personally but within the work environment as well. Philippians 4:6 tells us to not worry about anything, but pray about everything. The Lord wants to hear about our joys, petitions, and fears. If we as Christians are meant to be citizens of Heaven, should we not immolate the God we serve and seek to hear from those around us? This may lead to difficult conversations that you may not want to hear, point out items that you may not have been aware of, or finally address issues that you were choosing to ignore, but open dialogue allows for a fluid exchange of ideas to improve not only the work environment but personal relationships as well. Strong communication leads to trust and better productivity. If someone can trust you with the small things, they can trust you with the large things.

Action items for improved delegation:

1. Delegate more responsibilities to your staff. I know this may go against many type A individuals that would like to make sure that things are done their way on their own schedule, but even God said it was not good for Adam to be alone and create a helper for him. Leaders must understand that they have valuable assets on their team that you may or may not know of. I recall being hired for a position because my experience in the IT realm stood out to them as an asset to their team because I could communicate effectively with external stakeholders and developers. There was also an instance where a procedural change was to be implemented across the region and marketing

materials were needed for our local offices. I took the initiative of creating fliers to present the message and shocked my supervisor who didn't know I also obtained a degree in digital media. Circling back to fundamentals of communication, talk to your employees to see what hidden talents or hobbies they may possess that can benefit the team, company, and your workload as a whole. You could be giving an employee the chance to shine in their wheelhouse, as well as empowering them to lead in different avenues.

2. Divide your team into three groups; early adopters, late responders, and those who go with the flow. This will help you when it comes to policy and procedural changes that need to take affect. Utilize the early adopters, people who are excited about change and eager to learn, to help you train and motivate the others. Moses had to utilize the Hebrew priest to get the rest of the nation on board with leaving Egypt upon his return from Midian. He also utilized Joshua and Caleb to remind the Israelites that if God brought the nation through the wilderness after 40 years, He would give the land of Jericho into their hands without fail. By placing trust in these individuals, you not only boost their self esteem, but build a stronger team who abhors the status quo and can't wait for the next challenge.

Action items for improved courage:

1. Courage is an internal asset that will require some digging and removal of toxic traits. Upon starting your day, before checking your phone for notifications, sit in the stillness of the morning and thank God for waking you up. This simple act of stillness, recognition, and acknowledgment is so powerful because it grounds you in His presence and gives you the

confidence to ask for guidance and peace throughout your day. Knowing that if He can wake you up and allow you to see another day, nothing you go through is too hard for Him to do. Release the fear and hold onto the promise that He has everything under control, and no matter where you go, all things are working out for your good.

2. Seek therapy. Yes we should seek God for guidance, but just as He allowed us to have doctors to treat medical emergencies, we also have clinicians for mental emergencies as well. Everyone reading this book has dealt with trauma whether it be family related, relationships, or undiagnosed anxiety and to be an effective leader, we must calm the storm within ourselves before we can assist with the rain surrounding us. Moses was torn between his desire to fit in with his adopted family or his biological community, resulting in his murdering of a guard and a life on the run. When called upon to do God's will, he gave every excuse not to take on the burden because he did not feel worthy. He was worthy...and you are worthy. Whether you know your trauma or just don't feel right about something you can't quite put your finger on, seeking a therapist can open up your heart, your eyes, and your perspective that you are human, you make mistakes, you are still loved, and at the end of the day...God continues to choose you.

Action items for improved vision:

1. Habakkuk 2:2 shares that we should write the vision down and make it plain, so that even on the run we can read it. So that goes without saying, write your vision down. It doesn't have to be a vision board with cut outs of magazine clippings, but write down where you wish to see yourself in a year, five years, or ten years. When you've written your personal goals, turn and write down your business goals. Where do you see your team going

this year? What are their career goals as it relates to your mentorship? Take out three sheets of paper and write down your personal goals, your team's goals, and your company's goals. Place them where you can see them everyday; on a dry erase board, laminated on your bathroom mirror, even your desktop's background. As long as you can see it, memorize and utilize it for guidance each day to help you down your road to success.

2. Now that you've written down your vision, it is imperative that you pray over it. Moses was in the wilderness and had moved on from his life in Egypt; marrying Miriam, having children, and even changed professions...until God shook it up. We might have an idea of where we want to go in life and how we would like things to go, but God can change it all in a moment and push you to fulfill the purpose He has for you, as Proverbs 19:21 expresses so eloquently, "many are the plans in a person's heart, but it is the Lord's purpose that prevails". Have faith, work towards a goal, but seek God's blessing over it to ensure that it's the right path you should be on. You'll know you received confirmation on your journey because when you come to a hard place and don't see any way forward, God will make a way out of no way just as He did with the various miracles upon Egypt, the Red Sea, in the wilderness, and more. Our God is faithful and if it is His will, He will provide provision for it.

Action items for improved sacrifice:

1. You've prayed, written the vision down, and put in the work...now learn to let go of control. The reason you must learn to delegate, go to therapy, and seek God's face is because though your part may be done in one season, that doesn't mean that God won't use you in another season and you have to gain the spiritual maturity to be ok and trust the process. I

39

can imagine how upsetting it was for Moses to face his fears and come back to Egypt after so long, lead an unruly group through the desert, make it to the gates of the promise land, only to not be let in. He could have stopped leading once he was told that he wouldn't cross over, but he continued to push through and perform at the best of his ability and train up Joshua in the way he should go. Moses knew that the bigger picture was not about his immediate fulfillment, but that the destiny of an entire nation was more important. The destiny of your team and your company is more important than one individual. As a leader you will weep, cry out in pain, falter in judgement, and possibly lose some of your best employees, but the mission, vision, and purpose of the team must and will prevail. A true leader will trust the process and trust the Lord through it all because as Romans 8:28 tells us, "all things work together for the good of them that love God, to them who are called according to his purpose."

I wish you many blessings on your quest to lead in a better and Godly fashion. As I release this, I pray that each of you that picks up this manuscript will gain the insight and guidance that God has for you. James 4:10 says to "humble yourselves before the Lord, and He will lift you up." The Lord who commands the winds and the waves is with you every step of your journey and sees your quest to better yourself for the empowerment and growth of those around you. Have faith and don't lose heart when trials come, for if you were called to this position, He will surely guide you through the uncertainty. I wish you a blessed and fruitful life full of success, in Jesus' name, Amen.

www.ingramcontent.com/pod-product-compliance
Lightning Source LLC
Chambersburg PA
CBHW031635040426
42452CB00007B/833